D1175088

DATE DUE		Metro Litho Oak Forest, IL 60452
FEB 01 1997	JUL 16 1999	
FEB 21 1997		
NOV 24 1997	DEC 13 1999	
	JAN 03 2000	
DEC 08 1997	JAN 03 2000	
MAR 09 1998	JUN 28 2000	
DEC 14 1998	OCT 18 2000	
JAN 06 1999	NOV 07 2000	
	JUL 02 2001	
FEB 20 1999		
MAR 29 1999		
JUN 22 1999		

91190

JB   Zadra, Dan
CRO   Davy Crockett

14.95

WE
THE PEOPLE
DAVY CROCKETT

Published by Creative Education, Inc. 123 South
Broad Street, Mankato, Minnesota 56001

Library of Congress Cataloging-in-Publication Data

Zadra, Dan.
    Davy Crockett : frontier adventurer, 1786-1836 / Dan Zadra ;
illustrated by Jack Norman.
        p. cm. — (We the people)
        Summary: A brief biography of the Tennessee woodsman renowned as a
hunter, scout, politician, and soldier.
        ISBN 0-88682-195-9
        1. Crockett, Davy, 1786-1836—Juvenile literature.   2. Pioneers—
Tennessee—Biography—Juvenile literature.   3. Legislators—United
States—Biography—Juvenile literature.   4. United States.
Congress.   House—Biography—Juvenile literature.   5. Tennessee—
Biography—Juvenile literature.   [1. Crockett, Davy, 1786-1836.
2. Pioneers.   3. Legislators.]   I. Norman, Jack, ill.   II. Title.
III. Series.
F436.C95Z33   1988
976.8′04′0924—dc19
[B]
[92]   87-33205
                                                                          CIP
                                                                          AC

WE
THE PEOPLE
DAVY CROCKETT

FRONTIER ADVENTURER
(1786-1836)

DAN ZADRA

Illustrated By Jack Norman

CREATIVE EDUCATION

DAVY CROCKETT

David Crockett was born in Greene County, Tennessee, in 1786. Legend says that little Davy learned to shoot before he even learned to

walk or talk. It's said that he could outrun a deer, stare down a bear, and whittle a tree stump into a riverboat with his pocket knife. These are all tall tales, of course.

The truth is, young Davy Crockett was a lot like any other young boy who grew up in the Tennessee backwoods. By age eight, a boy had usually learned to hunt for his supper. Girls, too, were expected to grow up quickly on the American frontier. It

was not unusual for a girl to marry at thirteen, have her first child a year later, and become a grandmother while still in her twenties!

Like most frontier families, the Crocketts were desperately poor. They mainly lived off the land, relying on wild fish and game. Mr. Crockett had tried being a farmer and a miller but had failed. Then he opened a small inn.

When Davy was 12, his father

hired him out to a passing traveler. The man needed a herd-boy to help with his cattle. He was going to Virginia.

Davy walked 400 miles, prodding cows all the way. Then he talked some kindly wagon-drivers into bringing him home.

His father sent him to school. But Davy only got into trouble and soon ran away. He hired out to another cattleman and started wandering all over Virginia and Maryland, taking odd jobs when he could. When he had no job, he roamed the woods. Deer meat made a tasty meal. Coonskin made a pretty good hat.

After two footloose years he came home and did farm work to help pay the family's debts. But the wandering spirit was still in him and it would be there until the day he died.

In 1804, when he was 18, Davy married Polly Finley. He tried farming for awhile, but what he really loved was hunting. He was the best shot in Tennessee—and everybody knew it.

The Crocketts had two children. Then Davy's wandering itch took over and he moved his family westward to the Elk River. It was wild

country, the kind Davy liked best. Inside of a year, he had killed 105 bears. People began to spin yarns about his hunting abilities.

"I heard-tell Davy kilt a grizzly with his bare hands," said one.

"I heard-tell he kilt two bars with a single bullet," said another.

Davy just smiled. He loved to hear stories about himself—even the ones that weren't quite true!

In 1813, Davy heard some exciting news. The Creek Indians were on the warpath. And General Andy Jackson was raising an army to go after them. Davy volunteered to be a scout. Polly wept and begged him not

to go, but his mind was made up.

The Creek warriors had been stirred up by the great Indian leader, Tecumseh. The red men feared that the whites would soon drive them from their homeland. It was a fear that came true only too soon.

Andrew Jackson hated the Indians. But his chief scout, Davy

Crockett, came to admire them even as he fought them. After all, the Creeks were only fighting for their homes. Davy could understand that.

Davy fought in Alabama and Georgia. The army was often short of food and the men welcomed the wild game Davy brought in. Once again, tall tales were spread about the man in the coonskin cap. As always, Davy just winked and smiled—and let the rumors fly.

Davy and some men went south into Florida and fought the Indians there. Then the war ended. Davy was glad. "I never liked this business with the Indians," he said later. He went home to Polly and took up his farmer's life once more.

For a few years he was happy.

Then Polly died. Davy was left with
two young sons and a baby girl. After
a time he married Elizabeth Patton, a
widow with two children whose hus-
band had died in the war.

Now the old restless feeling laid hold of Davy again. He moved from place to place—never satisfied. About 1820 he went to far western Tennessee. There, by the Mississippi river, he settled down near Reelfoot Lake. It was a lonely, mysterious land. The lake itself had been created by a monstrous earthquake in 1811. Sometimes the ground still trembled as Davy planted corn.

If there was anything Davy loved better than hunting, it was telling tall tales and funny stories. In those days, there were no radios or television. Even newspapers were rare. A story-teller like Davy was a valued citizen. And the folks in Tennessee knew Davy not only as a man with a glib tongue, but also as a war hero and "the best darned bear hunter in the West."

So, in 1821, they nominated him to the legislature.

Davy Crockett served the people well. He continued to tell the colorful backwoods tales that were his trademark. Soon his fame spread even beyond Tennessee. People began to talk about sending him to Congress in Washington.

In 1827, when the next election was held, David Crockett was elected Representative from the district of western Tennessee.

People called him the "Coonskin Congressman." Though he now wore ordinary city clothes, he still held on to his pioneer shrewdness, his backwoods honesty, and his ability to

smell out a phony. Up to this time, most congressmen had been wealthy and educated men. But Crockett was a "man of the people" who proved he could beat the fancy politicians at their own game.

In 1833, he was re-elected for a second term.

He fought for the rights of small homesteaders, who were being driven from their lands by rich men. He became a champion of the southeastern Indians, who were driven from their lands by the whites. President Jackson, who had been Crockett's friend, turned against him. Crockett's bills on behalf of the poor farmers and the Indians were defeated. By now, he had made many political enemies. When Davy ran for

re-election in 1835, he too was defeated.

Davy's life in politics was fizzling to a close in Washington. But the legend of Davy Crockett was still

25

shooting like a skyrocket across the land. Between the years 1835 and 1836, fifty pamphlets called "Crockett Almanacs" were published in America. The pamphlets contained exciting stories—true and untrue—about the doings and sayings of Davy Crockett, Daniel Boone, Kit Carson and other frontier heroes. These pamphlets helped build a few rugged frontiersmen into "legends" bigger than life.

Meanwhile, Davy had gone off to Texas in search of a new adventure. He arrived there just in time to join a war.

English-speaking Texans had decided to break free of Mexico and form a republic. Mexico had sent a large army to punish the Texas rebels.

At that time, early in 1836, only one fort stood in the path of the Mexican army. It was the old Alamo mission at San Antonio. Crockett hurried to join in its defense. He was welcomed by William Travis, its young commander, and Jim Bowie, a famous adventurer.

On February 22, 1836, an army of about 3,000 Mexican troops led by General Santa Anna surrounded the little fort.

Davy and the other 186 defenders of the Alamo held out for 12 days, hoping that reinforcements would soon arrive. On the morning of March 6 the Mexican army stormed the Alamo walls. Fighting hand to hand, the Alamo defenders died to the last man. Davy Crockett's

coonskin cap lay in the rubble alongside his body. The brave frontiersman was gone, but his legend would live on.

"Remember the Alamo!" The cry rang out all over Texas. A few weeks later, an American force led by Sam Houston defeated Santa Anna and his army near the San Jacinto River. Davy Crockett had not died in vain. The republic was free at last.

WE THE PEOPLE SERIES

WOMEN OF AMERICA

CLARA BARTON
JANE ADDAMS
ELIZABETH BLACKWELL
HARRIET TUBMAN
SUSAN B. ANTHONY
DOLLEY MADISON

INDIANS OF AMERICA

GERONIMO
CRAZY HORSE
CHIEF JOSEPH
PONTIAC
SQUANTO
OSCEOLA

FRONTIERSMEN OF AMERICA

DANIEL BOONE
BUFFALO BILL
JIM BRIDGER
FRANCIS MARION
DAVY CROCKETT
KIT CARSON

WAR HEROES OF AMERICA

JOHN PAUL JONES
PAUL REVERE
ROBERT E. LEE
ULYSSES S. GRANT
SAM HOUSTON
LAFAYETTE

EXPLORERS OF AMERICA

COLUMBUS
LEIF ERICSON
DeSOTO
LEWIS AND CLARK
CHAMPLAIN
CORONADO